EMOTIONAL HEALTH ISSUES

Self-harm
and Suicide

Jillian Powell

WAYLAND

First published in 2008
by Wayland

Copyright © Wayland 2008

Wayland
338 Euston Road
London NW1 3BH

Wayland Australia
Level 17/207 Kent Street
Sydney, NSW 2000

Series editor: Nicola Edwards
Consultant: Peter Evans
Designer: Alix Wood
Picture researcher: Kathy Lockley

The case studies in this book are based on real experiences but the names we have used are fictitious and do not relate to real people. Except where a caption of a photograph specifically names a person appearing in that photograph, or an event in which real people have participated, all the people we have featured in the book are models.

The author and publisher would like to thank the following for allowing their pictures to be reproduced in this publication:
Ace Stock/Alamy Images: 17; Mark Baigent/Alamy Images: 23; Paul Baldesare/Photofusion Picture Library: 10; Mark J. Barrett/Alamy Images: 25; Jaubert Bernard/Alamy Images: Cover, 21; George Blonsky/Alamy Images: title page, 36; Trygve Bolstad/Panos Pictures: 42; Bubbles Photolibrary/Alamy Images:15, 19; Comstock Select/Corbis:13t; Simon Cowling/Alamy Images: 4; Jo Giron/Corbis: 35; Richard Green/Alamy Images: 7; Steve Hamblin/Alamy Images: 40; Ute Klaphake/ Photofusion Picture Library: 24; Kolvenbach/Alamy Images: 26; Mediscan/Corbis: 34; Charlie Newham/Alamy Images: 8; Christian Schmidt/zefa/ Corbis: 32; Tom Stewart/Corbis: 38; Thinkstock/Corbis:13b; Jim West/Alamy Images: 44; David White/Alamy Images: 14; Terry Whittaker/Alamy Images: 45; Janine Wiedel Photolibrary/Alamy Images: 37; Wayland Archive: 16, 20, 28, 30

British Library Cataloguing in Publication Data

Powell, Jillian
   Suicide and self-harm. - (Emotional health issues)
   1. Suicidal behavior - Juvenile literature 2. Parasuicide -
   Juvenile literature
   I. Title
   362.2'8'0835

ISBN: 978 0 7502 4767 2

Printed in China

Wayland is a division of Hachette Children's Books,
an Hachette Livre UK company.

Contents

Words that appear in **bold** can be found in the
glossary on page 46.

Introduction

Jemma has been cutting her arm again. She uses the blade from a razor. Jemma doesn't know why she cuts herself. She just knows that the feeling builds and builds inside her until cutting is her only release. When she is cutting, she feels as if she can breathe again. Afterwards, she feels ashamed and guilty. She has to wear long sleeves to hide the cuts on her arms.

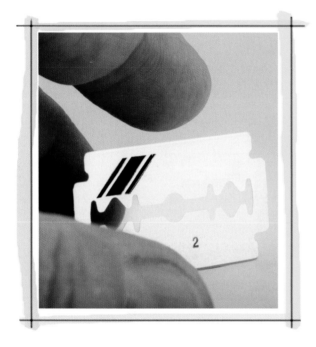

Razor blades are sometimes used for cutting, a practice that carries with it a risk of infection.

Jemma is self-harming. Self-harm means deliberately hurting or injuring oneself. It can take many forms, such as cutting, scratching or burning the skin, pulling out hair or eyelashes, or punching and bruising oneself. Other forms of self-harm include deliberately engaging in risky behaviour, such as practising unsafe sex, smoking or drinking heavily, **inhaling** substances and **overdosing** on **prescribed** or illegal drugs.

Suicide

Suicide is also increasing among children and teens. In the UK it is now the second leading cause of death (after accidents) in young people. In a third of all countries, young people are the highest risk group for suicide. In Britain, the charity ChildLine receives 1,500 calls a year from children who are thinking about suicide, some as young as six. Although girls are more likely to attempt suicide than boys, boys are more likely to die by suicide.

Coping with emotions

Suicide and self-harm are very different, although they are related.

Both are ways of dealing with very strong emotions. Both reflect a feeling of low self-worth. But self-harm is not usually an attempt at suicide. Rather, it is an attempt to cope with feelings of pain and distress. Suicide can be a reaction to feelings of hopelessness and despair. It is a way of bringing to an end feelings that are too painful to bear. Although many people self-harm for years without attempting suicide, suicide can sometimes follow self-harm. People with a long-term habit of self-harm are at greater risk of attempting suicide.

Self-harm

In the past three decades, self-harm has become more common among children and young people. Statistics from around the world suggest that as many as one in ten young people self-harms. Actual figures may be even higher, because many cases go unreported. Self-harm is most common among teens. The average age at which someone starts self-harming is between 12 and 14, but self-injury has been reported in children as young as four.

Find out more

This book gives you the facts about self-harm and suicide. It explains the causes and risk factors for self-injury and suicide, and identifies the impacts on young people and their families.

The book considers why self-harm and suicide are increasing among children and teens, offers advice on ways to seek help, and shows that young people can overcome problems and learn to find other means of coping with crises in their lives.

It's a fact: self-harm and suicide

- About one in ten teenagers self-harms.
- In the UK, three teenagers self-harm every hour.
- Around 500,000 people in the UK self-harm.
- Around three million Americans, most of them adolescents, self-harm.
- Around 6000 people die by suicide in the UK each year.
- Each year, about 32,000 Americans die by suicide. Almost 5,000 of them are under the age of 24.
- Each day in the United States, 14 people aged 15 to 24 die by suicide – approximately one every 100 minutes.

Chapter 1: *Depression and mental disorders*

Both self-harm and suicide reflect underlying problems of depression. Most people feel sad or depressed sometimes. Feeling sad is normal when a person experiences events that are upsetting or stressful. During **puberty**, feelings and emotions are affected by chemicals in the body called **hormones**. These chemicals can alter mood, sometimes causing mood swings and making a young person feel sad and tearful, or angry and upset.

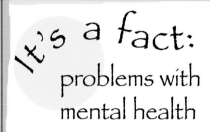

It's a fact: problems with mental health

- One in four people worldwide will have mental health problems at some time in their lives.
- Serious emotional disturbances affect one in every ten young people at any given time.
- One in eight teens suffers depression.

Temporary mood swings are normal, and usually pass. But when depression goes on for months and begins to affect home and school life, a young person may need help and treatment. Some teens are more likely to develop depressive illnesses because of genetic factors. External stresses – things that are happening in their lives that make them feel unhappy or anxious – can combine with **genetic** factors to lead to **major depression**, an illness which requires treatment.

Rising mental health problems

Recent studies show that cases of depression and other mental disorders are increasing in children and young people. The World Health Organization (WHO) and the United Nations

Children's Fund (UNICEF) recently warned that up to one in five of the world's children has mental health or behavioural problems. This includes children living in developed countries as well as in developing nations and war zones.

A greater number of girls than boys have emotional disorders, such as **eating disorders**. More boys have behavioural disorders, such as **attention-deficit/hyperactivity disorder (ADHD)**. Some mental disorders are temporary; others can become long-term problems that lead to academic failure, self-harm, alcohol and drug abuse and suicide.

Anti-depressants

Doctors have been prescribing an increasing number of children and young people with drugs called **anti-depressants**. These drugs affect mood by altering the balance of chemicals in the brain. Some have recently been banned for under-18s because scientific research has shown they may increase suicidal feelings in children and young people. But others are still being prescribed for tens of thousands of children every year. A recent survey found that 85,000 children in the UK were taking anti-depressants.

Some people claim that the rise in the number of children and young people being diagnosed with depression and other disorders is a result of better methods of diagnosis and improved understanding of mental health. Others believe that the increase reflects the growing pressures and stresses on young people today.

Social changes and causes

Being a child today is very different from being a child in previous generations. Many experts believe that the rise in depression and mental health problems among children is due to new stresses and pressures they face. These stresses come from changes in society and the family as well as from pressure at school. Another source of stress comes from the influence of a range of media, such as magazines, television and the Internet.

Changes in the family

In the United Kingdom, where one in three marriages ends in divorce, nearly one in four children lives in single-parent families. Although many children grow up without problems in lone-parent households, they are twice as likely to have mental health problems as children in two-parent families. This may reflect the difficulties that some parents have coping alone with the financial and other challenges this brings. In the United States, where about half of all marriages end in divorce, one study found that 20 to 25 per cent of children suffered long-term depression after their parents' split. Children living in stepfamilies are also much more likely to suffer depression and mental health problems.

Exam pressures

At school, children face increased academic pressures. In many countries, students are being tested at younger ages than ever before. Student surveys indicate that academic pressure is one of the greatest sources of stress among teens. The admissions procedure for colleges and universities has grown more competitive, and young people are struggling to achieve high

An increasingly competitive job market puts young people under more pressure to gain qualifications.

CASE STUDY

Thirteen-year-old Lauren had been feeling unhappy since her parents divorced when she was eleven. She still cried when she thought about the day they told her of their decision. Although she got to see her dad most weekends, she missed him terribly. Things got worse at home when her mum's new boyfriend, Daniel, moved in. He was much stricter than her dad, and grounded Lauren for the smallest offence. Lauren resented Daniel because he was not her dad; she felt Daniel was trying to take her father's place. Her mum always seemed to take Daniel's side, making Lauren feel like an outsider in her own home. Her mum didn't understand how Lauren felt, and Lauren dared not tell her dad because she didn't want to cause more trouble between her parents. She started having headaches and stomach-aches, and began missing school. With exams coming up, Lauren was feeling under pressure. Her marks had been sliding, and her teacher was disappointed in her performance. Lauren felt that everything in her life was spinning out of control. She called a children's helpline because she felt desperate to talk to someone.

standards of performance. They worry about meeting their parents' and their own expectations.

Bullying

Bullying is a major problem in many schools. With the growth of Internet use among children, bullying also now occurs through text messages, in e-mails and on websites. One in seven children in the United States, or approximately five million, is affected as either bully or victim. In the UK, bullying is the most common reason for calls to ChildLine. Here, one in five cases of suicide in children and young people is as a result of bullying. Constant bullying causes low self-esteem, which is a major factor in self-harm and suicide. Sometimes it can be the last straw for a young person who may be facing other problems, such as family break-up or bereavement.

Teen consumers

Children and teens are often targeted as consumers by advertisers. Media images show slim and glamorous models. Young people, whose bodies are changing during puberty, can experience low self-esteem and develop poor body images when they feel they do not measure up to media portrayals. Images of ultra-thin models and celebrities can encourage healthy young girls to feel that they are overweight, and may contribute to eating disorders such as **anorexia nervosa** and **bulimia nervosa**.

Chapter 2: *Self-harm: the facts*

Self-harm is also called self-injury. There are many different ways in which people deliberately harm themselves (see page 4). The most common way people self-harm is by cutting. Usually they cut their arms or legs, but they may cut any part of the body, such as the face or chest.

Self-harm methods

Most self-harmers use knives, razor blades, glass or other sharp objects. Sometimes they scratch the skin with fingernails, combs or knives, or deliberately pick at scars to open wounds again. Burning or scalding the skin is another type of self-harm, usually using cigarettes and matches.

Some people scrub their skin with substances like bleach, or pull out their hair or eyelashes. Others self-harm by banging their heads or throwing themselves against walls hard enough to bruise themselves. They may punch or hit themselves, or press painfully hard on to their eyeballs. Some may even break bones in their

Young people often feel immune to risks and deliberately rebel against health warnings.

arms or legs using bricks or hammers. Another form of self-harm is the practice of swallowing or inhaling dangerous substances.

Risky behaviour

People can also self-harm through deliberately risky behaviour. Risky behaviour can be a way of trying to block out anxiety or unhappiness by providing relief, if only temporarily, from unwanted feelings. This can be seen in recent trends which show that young people are experimenting with new and dangerous extreme sports, such as 'tombstoning' – jumping into the sea from high cliffs – or 'car surfing' – jumping on to the top of moving vehicles. Young people also take risks by practising unsafe sex without using condoms and sometimes with a number of different partners. This behaviour increases the risk of contracting sexually-transmitted infections and diseases, including **human immunodeficiency virus (HIV)**, which is the virus that causes **acquired immune deficiency syndrome (AIDS)**.

People who self-harm may also smoke heavily or engage in **binge drinking**, putting their health at risk. Using drugs recklessly is another form of self-harm. Drug overdoses are the most common cause of hospital admissions for self-harm. Many self-injurers have co-existing problems of substance abuse, **obsessive-compulsive disorder (OCD)**, or eating disorders.

CASE STUDY

Sophie was fourteen when she started self-harming. She was at a big family gathering after her grandmother's funeral. Sophie had adored her grandmother and had often gone to her house after school to chat. She felt Nan was the one person whom she could tell anything. While other family members and friends were talking and eating, Sophie locked herself in the bathroom upstairs. She noticed a disposable razor lying on the side of the bathtub, and something made her pick it up and cut the back of her hand. Somehow she felt that she was shutting out everyone else at the funeral, and every event that was happening. Seeing her own blood made her feel more real and alive. The physical pain came as a relief to the heartache she had been feeling since her grandmother's death. Sophie didn't tell anyone about the cutting, but she soon did it again. She began locking herself in the bathroom and pretending to take long baths. She was becoming addicted to the rush and the relief that she remembered from the day of her grandmother's funeral.

Who self-harms?

People of every age, race and background can self-harm. Women and girls are more likely to self-harm than men and boys. However, instances of self-harm among men and boys have doubled since the 1980s. The rates are highest among young people.

Young women between the ages of 15 and 19 are most at risk of practising self-harm, as are young men between the ages of 20 and 24 years. Self-harm is also becoming more common in children. In the United Kingdom, more

Self-harming sessions are often 'time out' for young people. They usually take place in private, in bathrooms or bedrooms.

It's a fact:
self-harm

- A recent study of fifteen- and sixteen year-olds in England showed that girls are four times more likely to self-harm than boys.
- Young Asian women have higher rates of self-harm than other ethnic groups.
- Some studies suggest that young people who are gay or lesbian are more likely to self-harm.
- Young people who abuse alcohol or drugs such as cannabis and cocaine are more likely to self-harm than those who do not have substance-abuse problems.

than 60 per cent of young people calling ChildLine about self-harm are between the ages of 12 and 15. Twelve times as many girls as boys call the helpline. Some studies in the United States suggest that 16 per cent of high school students have self-harmed. College counsellors report growing numbers of students asking for help because they are self-harming, leading some mental health professionals to call it 'a hidden epidemic' among the young.

Some groups of young people are at greater risk of self-harm than others. Children with mental health problems or learning difficulties are more likely to self-harm, as are those who have experienced **physical abuse** or **sexual abuse**. Young people who are homeless, in foster care or in young offender institutions have higher rates of self-harm.

Overwhelming problems

People who self-harm are likely to be depressed and worried. They may be overwhelmed by the problems in their lives, and think that they are unable to cope. They may blame themselves for their problems and be unable to seek help from family or friends. Some people self-harm only once or twice, as a reaction to extreme stress or anguish. They might bang their heads or punch their fists against walls

because they feel angry and frustrated or upset. For them, self-harm can be a way of coping temporarily with problems or setbacks. But for others, self-harm can develop into a way of coping with their problems. It becomes something they do every week or even every day. For them it is a means of blotting out difficult circumstances or emotions that they are dealing with on an everyday basis. They may also turn to it when something triggers memories of a painful experience or event.

Self-harm can sometimes be an impulsive act, in response to sudden anger or frustration.

Why do some people self-harm?

Self-harm is a way of coping with very difficult or painful feelings. During cutting or burning, for example, people can experience a temporary relief or release from their bad feelings. They feel as if physical pain briefly blots out their mental pain. After self-harming, however, they often feel guilty and upset that they have resorted to harming themselves.

Feeling addicted

Self-harm can have different effects on different people. Some people say that the sensation of pain makes them feel aware and alive; it stimulates them out of depression, emotional numbness, apathy or hopelessness. Others say that they feel a sense of detachment when they self-harm. Self-harm is habit-forming. Some experts believe it may be physically addictive. When the body is injured, it releases painkilling chemicals. Often people who develop long-term self-injury behaviour find that they have to self-harm more often and more severely to achieve the same sense of relief they once did.

Experiencing abuse

Some people self-harm because they feel their behaviour gives them control and ownership of their bodies. This is often true of people who have been physically or sexually abused. Children who have been abused may feel that they have no control over what happened to their bodies. They may also feel a deep sense of shame and guilt that they were unable to stop the abuse, even though it was not their

The actress Angelina Jolie has spoken about cutting herself when she was a teen. She said that being teased and feeling rejected led to depression and then to self-harm.

fault. Abused children may feel disgust for their bodies. Self-harm becomes a form of punishment, or a way of expressing the disgust and guilt they have been made to feel.

Keeping self-harm secret

Once people begin to rely on self-harm, it can be hard for them to stop. They may feel guilty or ashamed and unable to talk about their behaviour. For this reason, self-harm is not usually a way of seeking attention from others. In fact, cutting and other forms of self-injury often remain hidden. Most people self-harm when they are alone and then hide any evidence that they have hurt themselves.

Some self-harmers have described it as a way of having their "own space". Others have likened it to "screaming silently; so no one else will hear". They see it as a way of dealing with their own problems rather than turning to others for help. They have control over the injuries and scars they are creating and see their behaviour as their secret alone.

Someone who is self-harming may choose to wear clothes that cover up the signs of injury, helping to keep the self-harm a secret from others.

In focus: expressing pain

The idea of expressing inner pain on the outside of the body can be traced to a long tradition in religion and ancient cultures. Wearing a hair shirt, uncomfortably rough to the skin, and covering the head or body with ash were once used to express deep feelings of shame or penitence. Some tribal peoples still use ash or body paint during periods of mourning to express the pain of bereavement and their feelings of grief.

What causes self-harm?

Self-harm is linked to low self-esteem. Self-esteem is how people think and feel about themselves. It is formed by the things that happen to them, and the way people behave towards them.

Self-esteem does not stay the same throughout people's lives. If a person's relationship ends, someone close to them dies, or they fail an exam, their self-esteem suffers. If they get good grades, and enjoy happy relationships with others, their self-esteem improves again. But some people feel bad about themselves all the time. They may feel that they are 'losers' and that others don't value or care for them. They may blame themselves for things going wrong or feel they have let others down. Low self-esteem can cause stress and worry and lead to depression. It can also lead to self-harm.

Low self-esteem can develop in someone who is criticized, ignored, teased or bullied regularly. For example, children who are constantly compared to high-achieving siblings may develop low self-esteem. They may worry constantly about letting themselves and their families down.

Bullying and abuse

Children and young people who have been bullied or abused are more likely to suffer low self-esteem. They feel that their opinions and emotions are not valued or important, and they often feel powerless to improve their situations.

A child may be bullied at school or at home, by a classmate, teacher, parent, step-parent, or sibling. The bully may focus on any number of characteristics – appearance, voice, race, religion or sexuality, for example.

Abuse can be emotional (such as name-calling and threats), physical or

Young people can bury the pain of abuse deep inside themselves, leading to feelings of loneliness and isolation.

sexual. Neglect, or failing to care for a child's basic needs such as clean clothes and adequate food, is the most common form of abuse.

Children and young people who suffer abuse are four times more likely than others to self-harm. They may feel that they can control or manage the pain of self-harm, unlike the pain they experience as a result of abuse.

Often children who are bulied at home can become bullies themselves at school, taking out their hurt and anger on others.

It's a fact: bullying

- Seven out of ten children have been bullied in school.
- One in ten teens has experienced online bullying.
- Girls are as likely to be bullied physically as boys.
- Bullying is the main reason children give for calling ChildLine.

Body image and self-harm

For most young people, body image is an important part of self-esteem. Body image is how people see themselves and how they think others see them. Surveys show that many children and teens are unhappy with their bodies. One in three teens would consider cosmetic surgery to improve their body shape. Although teenage girls are most affected, boys and young men are increasingly affected by poor body image. They compare themselves to idealized advertising and other media images and they feel under pressure to have similarly muscular and toned bodies. Polls show that children as young as six feel that they are overweight and need to diet. Two out of three girls under the age of 13 have been on diets. Children and teens who have physical disabilities or scars from accidents can also develop low self-esteem because of body image.

Celebrity icons

Many people believe that young people are becoming more concerned with body image because they are surrounded by images of celebrities and models looking ultra-slim and attractive. Children grow up believing others will judge them on how they look. If they feel they fail to measure up, their poor body image can lead to self-harm.

It's a fact: superskinny models

- Most photographs of fashion models are airbrushed to create an ideal but unrealistic appearance.
- Twenty years ago, models weighed eight per cent less than other women, on average; today, models weigh 23 per cent less than other women.
- Although 19 per cent of teenage girls are overweight, 67 per cent say they think they are too heavy.
- Teenage girls and young women make up 90 per cent of people with eating disorders.
- About 80 per cent of women say that they have low self-esteem after looking at fashion magazines.

Teenage girls can become obsessed with body weight, sometimes alternating between dieting and comfort-eating.

CASE STUDY

Michelle was always reading celebrity magazines and wishing she could look like her idols. She envied their figures and glossy looks. Michelle hated the way she looked. Since reaching puberty she had been getting spots and had noticed an increase in her body fat. She thought that all her mates were slimmer and better looking than she was. When they went out to clubs, she was always the one left standing on her own. The problem was, Michelle enjoyed food and just couldn't help eating for comfort when she was feeling down. Sometimes she would eat a whole box of sweets and then feel really upset and angry with herself. One night, Michelle overheard a boy call her 'the fat one'. She felt devastated. She didn't tell her friends, but she went home and cried. She hated herself and felt others hated her, too. Michelle began scratching her arms with pins because it felt like a way of punishing herself. In her mind, she was telling herself that it didn't matter if she got scars – she was so fat and ugly anyway.

Drugs and self-harm

Some people use alcohol or other drugs to self-harm. Most people admitted to hospitals for self-harm have taken drug overdoses. Young people, and those self-harming for the first time are more likely to take an overdose of an over-the-counter medicine, such as the painkiller paracetamol. Older people and people with a long-term habit of self-harm are more likely to overdose on prescribed anti-depressants or **tranquillizers**. One study in the United Kingdom showed that 14 per cent of 20- to 24-year-olds and seven per cent of 12- to 15-year-olds admitted to hospital for self-harm had taken illegal drugs before they were admitted to hospital. Young men were twice as likely as young women to have used illegal drugs to self-harm.

Half of all men and a quarter of all women admitted to hospital for self-harm had been drinking alcohol.

Alcohol abuse

Young people who abuse alcohol are more likely to self-harm. Under-age drinking is becoming a problem in many countries. It is illegal for under-18s to buy alcohol in the United Kingdom. In the United States, people younger than twenty-one are not legally allowed to drink alcohol. However, every year, thousands of 10- to 15-year-olds are admitted to hospitals for **alcohol poisoning**. Scientific studies in the United States show that young people who abuse alcohol risk long-term physical and mental damage. Yet more and more young people are regularly binge drinking (consuming five or more

Young people may get into difficulties when they do not realise the strength of the alcoholic drinks they are consuming. Alcohol poisoning can quickly lead to loss of consciousness and, if emergency treatment is not given, even to death.

In focus: overdosing

A drug overdose is the accidental or intentional use of a drug or medicine in an amount that is higher than is normally used. Even drugs generally considered safe can cause serious health consequences when taken in excessive amounts. Paracetamol (known as Acetaminophen in the United States) is an over-the-counter medicine used to reduce fever and relieve pain. Overdose of the drug can result in liver and kidney damage. The drug is the most common method of self-poisoning in the UK, especially among teenage girls and young Asian women.

The ready availability of painkillers makes them the most common means of self-poisoning.

alcoholic drinks within a short period). The findings of the National Survey on Drug Use and Health, released in 2005, indicated that more than 40 per cent of people aged 18 to 25 in the United States reported binge drinking at least once a month.

Drug abuse

Young people who abuse illegal drugs are also more likely to self-harm. Doctors believe that using drugs such as Ecstasy and marijuana can dull the brain's thinking and memory powers, and lead to physical and mental health problems. Young people are three times more likely than older people to become addicted when using

marijuana. Drug abuse can lead to mental health problems including panic attacks, **paranoia** and depression. Research also links drug use to the development of **schizophrenia**. Young people who abuse drugs and alcohol are also more likely to engage in high-risk behaviour such as unsafe sex, fighting, failure to use seat belts and riding in a car with a driver who has been drinking alcohol. In the United States in 2005, the National Survey on Drug Use and Health reported that the rate of treatment for young people with mental health problems who were abusing drugs was significantly higher, at 32 per cent, than the rate (19.3 per cent) for those who were not.

Youth subcultures

Many young people feel the need to belong to a smaller group or subculture within society. They express their personality or identity by banding together with others who like the same kind of clothing and music. Group identity can also include marking the body with **tattoos** and **piercings**. Some youth subcultures, such as Goths and emos, (fans of 'emotional hard core' bands) have been linked with high rates of self-harm and suicide. These subcultures can glamorize ideas of loneliness, unhappiness and death. Many scientists think that the subcultures attract self-harmers who can find support among peers to help them deal with their problems.

Self-harm and music

Recent studies suggest a link between self-harm and heavy metal, blues and emo music. Some emo bands show people cutting on their album covers. There is also a growing genre of self-harm lyrics and music. Goth rockers, such as Marilyn Manson, have been criticized for appearing to glorify self-harm. Manson, who cuts himself with broken glass on stage, is said to have hundreds of scars on his body from self-harm.

In focus: self-harm circles

Most people self-harm when they are alone. It is a private, even secret, activity. Some young people, however, belong to groups within or outside school who practise self-harm. The members send each other text messages when they have self-harmed and exchange pictures of scars. Some members even get together when they are cutting. Others join self-harm communities on the Internet and communicate through chat rooms or message boards.

Copycat behaviour

Some studies in Australia and the United Kingdom suggest that young people may be encouraged to engage in 'copycat' behaviour by hearing about celebrities or seeing familiar characters in television soap dramas self-harming. They are also more likely to self-harm if they know a relative or friend who does it.

Health care professionals have called for careful reporting of celebrities self-harming. They believe that teenagers who are going through a difficult time can be influenced by people they relate to, and may see self-harm as an appropriate way of dealing with their problems.

Self-harm websites

Many websites about self-harm offer a valuable source of information and support and a safe place for young people to chat with others who understand the feelings they are experiencing. Some people fear, however, that such sites make self-harming seem commonplace, and even encourage vulnerable young people to self-harm. Research has found that some message boards include content that might reinforce or promote self-harm. Members sometimes post pictures of their scars and other injuries. They exchange music tracks and poems about self-harm. Some websites even offer merchandise, such as T-shirts and bracelets, that expresses membership of a self-injury club.

Message boards and chat rooms provide a forum for young people to talk about others going through similar experiences.

Chapter 3: *Self-harm: treatment*

Most people who self-harm want to stop, but don't know how. They may feel that hurting themselves is the only way that they can cope with their feelings. But there are techniques that can help them prevent destructive behaviour. Identifying possible causes of emotional pain and triggers of self-harming behaviour can be valuable.

Some people find it helpful to keep a mood diary or journal. Writing down how they feel can help them see how various events affect their mood. Recognizing the events and feelings that can trigger self-harm is an important step towards stopping the pattern of behaviour.

Another beneficial exercise is to write down a list of reasons against self-harming. Scripting a dialogue can be useful, too, between one speaker who wants to self-harm and another who wants to stop.

Keeping a diary can provide an outlet for feelings and also help in recognizing patterns of thought and behaviour.

In focus: *seeing blood*

Many people who self-harm by cutting say that the sight of blood represents bad feelings and stress flowing out of their bodies. Others say the blood is a substitute for the tears they can't cry. When they bleed, they experience relief and calm. One self-help technique recommended by therapists is to mark the skin temporarily, for example with a lipstick.

Distractions

Distraction techniques can help some people avoid acting on the urge to self-harm. They might phone a friend, listen to music, go for a walk or exercise. Exercise and playing a sport can help, because those activities cause the release of natural **endorphins** in the body. Endorphins are substances in the brain that can improve mood.

Creative activities, such as writing poetry, painting and drawing, can act as an outlet for feelings. One way of expressing a strong emotion such as anger is to create an abstract painting of shapes or a self-portrait in blacks and reds.

Coping strategies

If feelings of anger and frustration build up, it can help to express them physically by punching into a pile of pillows or a punchbag. Another method is to use relaxation techniques, such as slow breathing, or counting from ten down to zero.

There are other ways of making the body feel 'harmless' pain too, such as holding an ice cube against the skin, letting an elastic band slap hard against a wrist or biting into a strongly flavoured food. Some people find it helps to mark their skin with a pen or stick plasters on the places on their bodies that they feel the urge to injure.

Taking part in sports can enhance mood as well as improving someone's physical health.

25

Getting help

Many people who self-harm need help and support to stop. Because self-harm can be a very lonely problem, it is important that young people talk to someone they can trust. The person could be a family member, friend, teacher, school counsellor, social worker or nurse. In many cases, they will be prepared to listen and give advice in confidence, but in circumstances where they think a young person may be in immediate danger, they will need to act on the information to see that he or she gets the help they need. Telephone helplines and support organizations also offer information and guidance.

Taking the first step

The first stage in getting help is often going to see the family doctor. Doctors will assess the seriousness of the problem and suggest a range of therapies, which may include

Telephone helplines can provide young people with immediate support and advice in times of crisis. Turn to page 47 for a list of helplines which people at risk of self-harm and suicide can contact.

In focus: peer support

Many young people feel more comfortable confiding in someone of their own age. In peer support groups, young people are trained by professional counsellors to listen in confidence to teens who face problems such as bullying, abuse and self-harm.

individual or family counselling, **psychotherapy** and medication to relieve anxiety and depression. Doctors generally provide emergency contact information that enables young people who repeatedly self-harm to seek psychiatric help during a crisis. If their self-harm behaviour becomes life-threatening, they may need to be hospitalized. Most hospital admissions for self-harm are for drug overdoses.

Therapy

Anti-depressants may be prescribed to relieve feelings of depression. In addition, anyone who self-harms needs to get help to deal with the problems that are causing his or her unhappiness. Some people may feel that they are to blame for everything that has gone wrong in their lives. They need help to change their way of thinking about themselves and about the events they have experienced in the past.

Young people with depression may be referred to counsellors, psychotherapists or psychologists who specialize in self-harm and problems such as abuse. Some of these people work at specialized clinics. They listen to teens and help them understand their feelings and manage them in a different way. These professionals may encourage young people to keep diaries and journals and to find other outlets for strong emotions and feelings.

It may also be helpful for a young person to join a self-help group locally or online, where people who share the same problems meet regularly to talk and help one another. Many young people feel more comfortable talking to their own peers. Peer support programmes in schools can offer a valuable source of help.

It's a fact:
recovery from self-harm

- Some people reach a point where they no longer feel the need to self-harm.
- Others find different coping strategies to help them through times of crisis.
- Talking with a trusted individual is the first step towards recovery.
- Most people who cut themselves aren't attempting suicide. It is possible for self-harm to result in accidental death, however, and it is also possible for suicidal and self-harming behaviours to co-exist in one person.
- People who self-harm regularly are more likely to attempt suicide than people who do not.

Family support

Many young people who self-harm try to keep their behaviour secret from their families. Often, they harm when they are alone, and they take care to hide the evidence with clothes. In some cases, a young person eventually confides in a family member. In other cases, parents or siblings accidentally discover the self-harm. They may see scars. Sometimes family members notice signs, such as clothing designed to cover up cuts or burns. Parents or siblings may find razors or knives hidden in bedrooms. They may accidentally catch the young person in the act of self-harm. Families can feel shocked, upset and bewildered when they uncover self-harming behaviour.

Someone to listen

A parent or sibling should not shout, become angry, judge or criticize a young person who is self-harming. If family members say the self-harmer is "crazy" or "stupid", the young person will feel more upset and alone. Issuing threats and extracting promises to stop self-harm behaviour are not helpful tactics. A child or teen who promises not to self-harm and then fails to keep that pledge may feel guilty and may be

Giving an ultimatum to a family member as a way of trying to stop self-harm can make that person feel more alone and less likely to confide in others.

CASE STUDY

When Amy's ten-year-old brother, Callum, found her self-harming, he felt worried and upset. Amy was alarmed that Callum had caught her cutting her arms, and she shouted at him for bursting into her room. Amy made him promise not to tell their mother about the cutting. Callum couldn't understand why Amy would want to hurt herself; she was clever, pretty and popular. He asked her why she was cutting herself, but she told him he was too young to be able to understand.

Callum felt awkward and embarrassed when their mother commented on Amy's long sleeves on a hot day. He felt torn. He knew that Amy was cutting herself when she shut herself away in her room. Callum knew that their mother would be angry if she learned that he hadn't revealed his sister's behaviour. Amy made him promise not to tell, though, and he was worried that telling his mother would cause more trouble in the family. One day, he saw an article about self-harm in a magazine. He decided to find out more information on the Internet. He found a lot of useful websites and printed some pages for Amy. He told her that she wasn't alone, and suggested that they should tell their mother together.

less likely to confide again. People who self-harm may feel worse if others try to force them to stop self-injuring or attempt to control their behaviour. Some self-harmers feel powerless or worthless and are trying to gain control over an area of their lives. They need help from people who will allow them to talk about how they are feeling and who will listen to them in a caring way.

Sometimes a brother or sister can help by offering to find out information, talk to an adult about the self-harm, or be with the sibling when he or she tells someone or seeks help. In some cases, a sibling may need to get first-aid help (such as wound care) for injuries. Serious injuries may need to be seen by a nurse or a doctor.

Family therapy

In some cases, doctors suggest family therapy. Therapy sessions include the young person as well as other members of the family. During family therapy, the child or teen can talk about his or her problems and unhappiness. The sessions help family members understand what is going on and work out ways in which they can make positive changes.

Chapter 4: *Suicide: the facts*

In general, suicide rates have been rising around the world, especially among the young. The World Health Organization reports a 60 per cent increase in suicides in the last 50 years. Some countries have much higher rates than others.

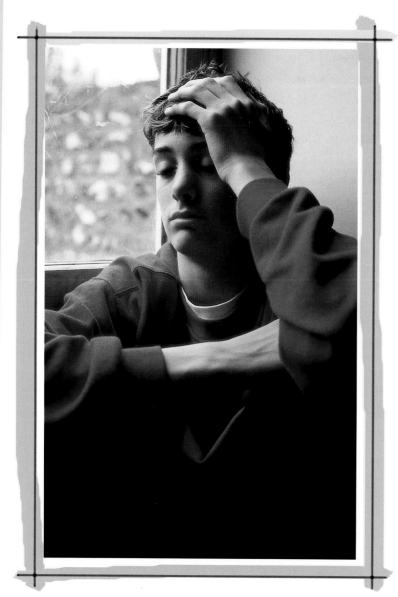

Teenage boys are among the highest-risk groups for suicide in many countries.

Rates of suicide

Finland and eastern European countries have the highest rates of suicide, with Japan, China, South Korea and Hungary also reporting high rates. Muslim countries, such as Jordan and Syria, where suicide is forbidden on religious grounds, have the lowest reported rates.

In the United States suicide is the third most common form of death, and a survey by the Samaritans in the United Kingdom lists suicide as the second most common cause of death (after accidents) among young people.

Girls are more likely to attempt suicide, but boys are more likely to die as a result.

It's a fact:
suicide

- Around 19,000 young people in the UK attempt suicide each year; 700 die as a result.
- Most suicide attempts are by drug overdose.
- Almost three out of four suicides are by males.
- Scotland has the highest suicide rate in the UK.
- Northern Ireland has the highest suicide rate among young men in the UK.

This may be because the most common method of attempted suicide by girls is by drug overdose, giving a chance of recovery if emergency treatment is given in time.

The rise of online suicide

The Internet has begun a new trend for group suicides among the young. In Japan, which has a high rate of suicide (almost 30,000 people a year) and a culture that believes suicide can be an honourable act, the number of 'Internet suicides' has recently more than doubled. Young people with suicidal feelings contact others on the Internet to plan and carry out group suicides, typically using poisonous substances or inhaling car exhaust fumes.

Feelings of despair

Young people who have attempted suicide report feelings of anxiety, loneliness and hopelessness. Low self-esteem and feelings of powerlessness or failure are common factors. Some have long-term depression; others have experienced **traumas**, such as family break-up or the death of a loved one.

Some young people were self-harming before they attempted suicide. Many report problems with parents, friends or the police. Some have experienced difficulties at school. Other factors include bullying and being bullied, unwanted pregnancy, sexual or physical abuse and poverty.

For someone who is feeling suicidal it can become impossible to reach out for help. Young people who are considering taking their own lives often have the false belief that others will be better off without them.

Who is at risk?

Some research suggests that half of all young people who attempt suicide have a history of self-harm. Other studies show that impulsive behaviour can be an important factor in suicides in this age group. In one study, a quarter of all suicides among young men were related to problems with close relationships in the days before their deaths.

Ethnic origins

Some groups of young people have higher suicide rates than others. Cultural and ethnic origins can be factors. A study in the United Kingdom found that suicide is three times as likely in young Asian women as in white British women. In the United States, the highest rates are found among non-Hispanic whites, American Indians and Alaska Natives. In those groups, stress can arise when a young person's wishes and expectations clash with the traditional values of their culture or religion.

Young people who live in rural areas in countries such as China and India also have high rates of suicide. They

There is a high incidence of mental health problems among young offenders, who are more than twice as likely to attempt suicide as adults in prison.

CASE STUDY

Nasreen's family moved to Britain from Pakistan before she was born. Nasreen and her family are Muslims, and religion is an important part of their lives. When she was 16 her parents told her they had arranged for her to marry her cousin, Nazir. Nazir was ten years older than Nasreen. When Nasreen told her parents that she had a boyfriend and did not want an arranged marriage, they threatened to throw her out of the house. If she did not agree to the marriage, they said, she would bring disgrace on her whole family. Nasreen's brothers made threats against her boyfriend and told him never to see Nasreen again. Her teachers began to notice that she seemed anxious and depressed. She did not want to dishonour her family, but she knew she could not marry a man she didn't love. Nasreen attempted suicide by taking an overdose of a painkiller. To her, suicide seemed to be the only way out.

may have difficulty finding work or homes. Southern India has the highest rate in the world for suicide among young people. Family or relationship conflicts and the breakdown of traditional family structures and support are thought to be factors.

Other high-risk groups

High rates of suicide have also been recorded among young people who are gay or lesbian. They may feel confused and isolated because of their sexuality. They may experience conflict within their families, bullying and even violence towards them.

Young people in prison or youth custody make up another high-risk group. In prison, people under the age of 21 have the highest suicide rate. Factors may include the existence of mood or behaviour disorders and bullying by other inmates.

A genetic link?

Some experts think that the presence of a sub-form of one **gene** makes impulsive behaviour and suicide more likely, but others disagree. Scientists in France and Switzerland recently reported that they had found a genetic variation which may be linked to suicide. Their research showed that the genetic alteration interfered with the brain's ability to produce a chemical that controls mood and anxiety levels.

Mood disorders and substance abuse

Overall, most suicides (90 per cent according to research) are linked to **mood disorders** or substance abuse. Young people who abuse drugs or alcohol have the highest suicide rates of any group, especially young males. One U.S. study of people under the age of 35 found that those with a history of drug abuse were five times as likely as others to die by suicide.

Underlying problems

Substance abuse is often the result of underlying problems, including depression and mood, personality or anxiety disorders. Taking drugs or alcohol is seen by some young people as a way of escaping difficult feelings. But alcohol and drugs can affect the ability to think and reason, and act as depressants, intensifying a mood of gloom and hopelessness. They also reduce inhibitions, making impulsive action more likely. The National Strategy for Suicide Prevention in the US estimates that between 40 and 60 per cent of those who die by suicide are **intoxicated** at the time. As many as one in five have used cocaine in the 24 hours before their death.

Reacting to trauma

Many young people who have mood, personality or anxiety disorders are

Young people can turn to substance abuse, such as inhaling solvents, to produce mind-altering effects and temporarily escape reality.

reacting to traumatic events in their lives. Some may have been physically or sexually abused. Others have gone through painful experiences such as family break-up. Young people who have a relative or friend who has committed suicide are also more at risk of suicidal feelings. They may be experiencing unbearable grief and an overwhelming sense of loss. There is also a risk of 'copycat' behaviour if they have strong feelings of wanting to 'join' a loved one, or feel that the loved one's death has somehow 'normalized' suicide.

CASE STUDY

Josh started taking drugs when he was 14. At school, a gang of bullies was picking on him and making his life miserable. He felt depressed most of the time. One day he was at a friend's house when he was offered marijuana. Josh smoked it because he wanted to find out what it was like. Smoking marijuana made him feel sick, but he also felt cool for doing it. He somehow felt that the bullies might respect him a bit more. Josh began to feel that smoking marijuana was a means of escape. It made him feel calm and confident.

Josh went with a friend to a club, where he met a dealer. Josh started buying cocaine and Ecstasy. He began to feel that getting high was the only good thing in his life, and he relied on drugs more frequently. At the same time, though, he felt more depressed. Josh was caught in a cycle that he thought he couldn't escape. Feeling trapped and hopeless, Josh took a drug overdose.

In focus: cluster suicides

In the United States, between one per cent and five per cent of suicides are 'cluster' suicides carried out by peer groups. These are a series of suicides that happen closely together in terms of time and place.

Some cluster suicides been inspired by an event or by a celebrity's suicide. For example, the death of rock star Kurt Cobain prompted a cluster of suicides among troubled fans. Cobain (1967-1994), lead singer of the U.S. rock band Nirvana, struggled with drug addiction. He was found dead at his home from a gunshot wound to the head.

Kurt Cobain

Suicide and anti-depressants

Drug therapy is one approach to the treatment of depression and suicidal thoughts and behaviour. Since the 1980s, anti-depressants have been prescribed to an increasing number of children and young people.

Brain chemicals

Depression is a result of many factors, which may include an imbalance of chemicals in the brain. Different factors, such as stress and the genes people inherit from their parents, can lead to

imbalances in these chemicals, which work to carry messages between the many millions of brain cells.

The brain chemical **serotonin** is important in controlling mood, emotions, sleep, and body temperature. If a person's brain has too much serotonin at any time, he or she may feel sick and get headaches. A low level of serotonin may cause a person to feel depressed, lack energy and appetite, sleep poorly, and take little interest or pleasure in things around them.

Careful monitoring

Some anti-depressant drugs, known as **selective serotonin reuptake inhibitors (SSRIs)** are thought to correct the imbalance of serotonin in the brain. Since being introduced SSRIs have been prescribed to millions of people around the world.

Recent studies have suggested that in some cases, these drugs can increase self-harming behaviour and suicidal throughts in adolescents. Some of them have since been banned for use in the under-18s. Doctors do still use some anti-depressant drugs alongside talking and other

Drugs can relieve the symptoms of depressive illness in the short term.

therapies, in cases of moderate to severe depression.

Doctors prescribe anti-depressants on a case-by-case basis, and are careful to assess patients regularly while they are taking them. Young patients are usually monitored every week during the first four weeks and regularly after that. They may need to continue taking anti-depressant medication for some months after they begin to feel better.

Drug therapies are not generally used for mild depression. In cases where they are used for young people, they are combined with other forms of therapy, such as counselling.

In focus: serotonin

The brain has many natural chemicals. The balance of these chemicals can be affected by hormones and genes, foods, alcohol and drugs. Levels of the 'mood chemical' serotonin can be reduced if someone is under stress, eats a poor diet, or has too little exercise, sleep or sunlight.

A well-rounded, nutritious diet and plenty of exercise, sleep and time spent outdoors may enhance a person's mood.

Drug therapies are always used alongside other forms of therapy, such as individual counselling and group therapy.

Chapter 5: *Suicide: prevention and therapy*

S ome experts estimate that 80 per cent of all people who attempt suicide want others to be aware of their intentions. In these cases, suicide may be called a 'cry for help'. In many countries, suicide prevention programmes train community workers, including school counsellors, social workers and religious leaders, to recognize the warning signs that someone has suicidal feelings. Doctors and nurses are also trained to identify and support those at risk of suicide.

Warning signs

Warning signs that someone may be considering suicide can include a range of symptoms:

- loss of interest in hobbies, school or work;
- neglect of personal care and appearance;
- giving away of prized possessions;
- depression or anger;
- withdrawal from friends and social activities;
- difficulties eating and sleeping;
- deliberately risky behaviour.

People with suicidal feelings may talk directly or indirectly about killing themselves. Sometimes they say they "want to end it all".

One-to-one counselling on a regular basis can provide an outlet for young people to talk about how they are feeling and prevent problems becoming overwhelming.

They may frequently mention death and dying, or the suicide of a famous person or someone known to them.

Getting help

People who show such symptoms need to speak with somebody who listens and encourages them to talk about their feelings. They may not have the mental or emotional energy to seek help alone, so they may need someone to act for them. Telephone-based crisis centres and helplines provide immediate support. Mental health professionals are also available to help.

Counselling and treatment

Often treatment begins with a visit to a family doctor. The doctor may then refer the young person to a specialist in mental health care. Children and teens who are suicidal may need counselling to get through a time of crisis.

Longer-term talking therapies encourage patients to deal with their negative feelings and behaviour. They explore the causes of negative feelings, and suggest appropriate techniques to manage them. Patients may also need to be referred for clinical treatment for alcohol or substance abuse.

Some troubled teens feel more comfortable talking to peer counsellors – young people who have been trained to support others of their own age who

In focus: taking action

The SOS (Signs of Suicide) Program in high schools in the United States has led to a 40 per cent reduction in suicide attempts in students exposed to the programme. Students are offered mental health check-ups and shown a video that helps them recognize depression and suicidal thoughts in themselves and their friends. The programme encourages them to 'ACT' (Acknowledge, Care and Tell).

If you have suicidal thoughts or think that someone you know may be feeling suicidal, take action now. Talk to someone you know and trust, or call a crisis helpline. Turn to page 47 for a list of organizations and people to contact.

are going through an emotional crisis and need guidance.

New strategies are also being developed to help prevent 'cluster' suicides (see page 35) and help young people cope with feelings of loss. These strategies can include one-to-one or group counselling, information packs and helplines. There are also calls for careful reporting of suicides, such as withholding details of the methods used to try to prevent copycat behaviour.

Suicide and the family

When people die by suicide, they leave behind family members and friends. These 'suicide survivors' have to come to terms with the tragedy. They experience many feelings associated with sudden bereavement, such as shock, disbelief, sadness, and anger. Suicide is especially difficult because a loved one has made the choice to die.

Family and friends may blame themselves and feel guilty because they didn't notice warning signs and weren't able to prevent the suicide. They may feel confusion and struggle to understand why their loved one chose to leave them. They may feel angry or hurt and betrayed. Sometimes people continue to have painful memories of finding the body or learning of the suicide.

Mourners at a funeral. When a person dies by suicide, it can be difficult for family and friend to come to terms with the knowledge that their loved one chose to die.

Dealing with grief

People sometimes find it hard to talk about suicide. Family members may respond differently, resulting in conflict or even family break-up. Surviving siblings may suffer because of their parents' preoccupation with the dead child. Siblings can become frightened and insecure, or feel that they are being overprotected by an anxious parent. Siblings may feel anger that a brother or sister has upset or even destroyed their family. Because people sometimes find it hard to talk about suicide in front of children, siblings can feel isolated. They may start to have physical symptoms, such as stomach-aches and headaches.

Coping strategies

It is important that everyone affected by a suicide is able to talk about their feelings openly. It is natural to feel sorrow, anger, and loss. Burying those strong emotions can lead to problems later, such as chronic tiredness, depression and even physical illnesses. Experts believe that this is because the body depletes itself using nervous energy to suppress strong emotions, rather than expressing them.

Keeping a journal and writing down feelings can be helpful. In addition to the support of family and friends, the help of a trained counsellor may be needed. Support groups enable survivors to meet others who have experienced the suicide of a family member or friend. Helplines and Internet chat rooms can offer contact and support, too. Some people benefit from becoming actively involved in a suicide prevention programme. They feel that helping others gives some meaning to their tragedy.

CASE STUDY

Darren was a conscientious student who worked hard at his studies. His goal was to become a doctor. When his girlfriend, Ellie, told him she had met someone else, Darren began to feel depressed and under stress. He worried about his performance in school and became overwhelmed by a feeling of all-round failure.

One day, when he was at home alone, Darren ended his life by suicide. He left a note for his parents and Ellie, saying that he was sorry he had let them all down and that they would be better without him.

Darren's parents were devastated that they had not known about his depression, and they blamed themselves. A police family liaison officer put them in touch with a suicide survivors' group. Darren's parents were helped by talking to other families who had gone through a similar tragedy.

Chapter 6: *Tackling the problem*

A ccording to the World Health Organization, mental health disorders are the fourth leading cause of ill health worldwide. The WHO predicts that depression will be the world's second biggest health problem by 2020.

A global problem

Self-harm and depression are becoming more common among children and young people. Changes in family and society appear to be a related factor. Modern society can be characterized by a lack of time and attention given by parents, and the replacement of outdoor and creative

In developing countries, poverty can be a cause of depression among young people.

play with entertainment from video and computer games. In some areas of the world, war, terrorism, poverty, and hunger are major causes of stress.

Developing countries

Young people living in rural areas face new problems, as traditional family and village structures break down and work becomes scarce. In many rural parts of developing countries, self-poisoning is a growing problem. About two-thirds of people who self-poison are younger than thirty. They may use agricultural **pesticides**, medicines, or natural poisons such as oleander seeds. In China, Malaysia, Sri Lanka, and Trinidad, 60 per cent to 90 per cent of suicides involve pesticide poisoning.

Working together

International organizations such as the European Union and the United Nations are working to raise awareness of the problems of suicide and self-harm. They want countries to work together to share resources and to consider the needs of children and young people in all mental health policies.

Some countries and states are considering new laws to restrict access to common methods of suicide. In

In focus: children's well-being

In 2007, UNICEF released a report on the well-being of children around the world. The report included findings on children's satisfaction in their relationships with their family and friends, feelings of safety, and enjoyment of school.

Among the twenty-one countries surveyed, Portugal, Austria, Hungary, the United States and the United Kingdom ranked lowest for children's well-being.

Canada, stronger laws on the handling and storage of firearms resulted in a decrease in suicide by firearms of almost 40 per cent. There are also calls for restrictions on package sizes of over-the-counter drugs (such as paracetamol) and for safer storage of pesticides. In places that attract suicides, such as bridges, the installation of emergency phones, fencing and nets may discourage people from jumping.

More research projects are also needed to study suicide and self-harm in children and young people. WHO has a World Suicide Prevention Day every year, which aims to raise awareness of this issue.

Supporting well-being

Young people today face many challenges in their lives that affect their physical and emotional health. Many factors, such as family break-up, are beyond their control. They can feel powerless to make changes, a situation that may damage their self-esteem.

Developing skills

Therapy for young people who self-harm aims to improve their self-esteem. It helps them find new ways of dealing with strong emotions and of controlling impulsive behaviour. Programmes develop problem-solving skills and help young people learn to communicate effectively with others.

Studies show that being in a supportive family and stable relationships reduces the risk of suicide and self-harm. The risk of suicide is also reduced by other factors, such as

- reducing access to weapons such as firearms;
- commitment to religious or spiritual beliefs, which may be accompanied by active participation in an organized religious community;
- involvement in community events;
- access to mental health care.

Building self-esteem

Having self-esteem helps a person deal with everyday stresses and problems. People can improve their self-esteem by setting realistic goals and giving themselves credit when they achieve them. Thinking positively and challenging their negative thoughts about themselves and events in their

Communication skills are not only important in making friends. They also allow people to build support networks which can be called on in times of trouble.

lives can also boost self-esteem. Some people are helped by recording in a journal or diary any positive events that happen during a day, such as completing a difficult task, performing well on a test, or receiving a compliment.

Self-esteem is improved by having positive role models and a network of supportive friends. Some people make a list of things that cheer them up, such as a pet, a friend, a favourite place or a happy holiday.

Other ways in which people can care for their physical and emotional health include exercising to release 'feel-good' endorphins, eating a healthy diet, and trying new activities and interests. People who take care of themselves and accept themselves as they are have taken the first step in avoiding self-harm.

Pets can provide companionship and unconditional love, enhancing a person's feeling of well-being.

In focus: *school programmes*

One strategy for improving well-being is through educational and counselling programmes in schools. These programmes are designed to help young people develop coping skills, especially in times of crisis. Some schools in the United Kingdom have introduced programmes to support children with depression. "A Place to Be" offers therapy through art, role-play, puppets, and storybooks. Children can also talk with a trained counsellor. The Penn Resiliency Programme operates in many countries including the United States. Teachers are trained to provide children with coping strategies, through exercises designed to build optimism and encourage long-term thinking and planning.

Glossary

acquired immune deficiency syndrome (AIDS) The final, life-threatening stage of infection with human immunodeficiency virus (HIV).

alcohol poisoning When the amount of alcohol in the blood becomes so high that the body is poisoned.

anorexia nervosa An eating disorder which starves the body of food.

antidepressants Drugs taken to treat depression by altering the balance of chemicals in the brain.

attention-deficit/hyperactivity disorder (ADHD) Disordered learning and disruptive behaviour which is characterized by inattentiveness, overactivity, or impulsive behaviour.

binge drinking Heavy, excessive drinking of alcohol.

bulimia nervosa An eating disorder in which a person has periods of eating uncontrollably (binging) followed by elimination of the food (purging).

eating disorders A range of eating problems caused by underlying emotional distress.

endorphins 'Feel-good' chemicals in the brain.

gene A very small part of a chromosome that influences inheritance and development of characteristics.

genetic Produced by genes.

hormones Chemicals made in the body that affect or control some body function.

human immunodeficiency virus (HIV) The virus that causes AIDS by damaging the body's immune system.

inhaling Breathing into the lungs.

intoxicated The state of being drunk, in which mental and physical control is diminished.

major depression Depression that has become a long-term illness.

mood disorders A range of problems that affect mood and well-being.

obsessive-compulsive disorder (OCD) A mental disorder in which a person has obsessive thoughts and engages in compulsive behaviour, such as repeated handwashing.

overdosing Taking an amount that exceeds a recommended or prescribed dose.

paranoia A mental disorder in which a person is overly suspicious that others are watching or talking about him or her.

pesticides Chemicals used in farming to kill pests.

physical abuse Physical mistreatment of a person by another.

piercings Body decorations made by piercing the skin for jewellery.

prescribed Ordered by a doctor as medicine or treatment.

psychotherapy Treatment of mental or emotional disorders by psychological means.

puberty The time during adolescence at which boys and girls become able to reproduce.

schizophrenia A mental disorder which can lead to a split personality.

selective serotonin reuptake inhibitors (SSRIs) A type of anti-depressant drug.

serotonin A chemical in the brain that is involved in controlling mood.

sexual abuse When a person forces somone into sexual acts or behaviour against their will.

tattoos Body decorations that are made using a needle and pigments.

tranquillizers Drugs that are given to people who are feeling anxious to make them feel calmer.

trauma An experience which has caused someone psychological pain.

Further information

Books to read

Craig Donnellan, *Self Harm and Suicide*, (Independence Educational Publishers 2000)

Claire Wallerstein, *Need to Know: Teenage Suicide*, (Heinemann 2004)

Dee Pilgrim, *Real Life Issues: Self Harm*, (Trotman Publishing 2007)

The Truth about Self-harm (Mental Health Foundation 2006)

Telephone helplines

ChildLine
A free helpline that young people in the UK can call to talk about any problem .
Telephone helpline: 0800 1111

Bristol Crisis Service for Women
A national voluntary organization for women in emotional distress.
Telephone helpline: 0117 925 1119

The Samaritans
Confidential emotional support 24 hours a day.
Telephone helpline: 08457 90 90 90

Sane
A helpline which is open every day from 1pm to 11pm for young people affected by mental illness and their families and carers.
Telephone helpline: 0845 767 8000

Helpful websites

www.selfharm.net

Lots of information on self-harm and therapies with links to other sites and resources.

www.youngminds.org.uk

The website for the national charity concerned with the mental health of children and young people. It has sections on suicide and self-harm.

www.selfharm.org.uk

An information resource for young people and their families. It has links to support organizations, counsellors and groups.

www.mentalhealthamerica.net

Comprehensive information including sections on self harm and suicide.

www.sane.org.uk

The website of the organization set up to offer information and help to people affected by mental illness and their families and carers.

Index